SPIRITUAL SAYINGS
OF
KAHLIL GIBRAN

THE BOOKS OF
KAHLIL GIBRAN

The Madman 1918
The Forerunner 1920
The Prophet 1923
Sand and Foam 1927
Jesus, the Son of Man 1928
The Earth Gods 1931
The Wanderer 1932
The Garden of the Prophet 1933
Prose Poems 1934
Nymphs of the Valley 1948
Spirits Rebellious 1949
A Tear and a Smile 1950
The Broken Wings 1959
The Voice of the Master 1960
A Self-portrait 1960
Thoughts and Meditations 1961
Spiritual Sayings 1963

Lazarus and His Beloved (play) 1973

A Treasury of Kahlil Gibran
edited by Martin L. Wolf 1974

SPIRITUAL
SAYINGS
OF
KAHLIL GIBRAN

Translated from the Arabic and edited by
Anthony R. Ferris

HEINEMANN : LONDON

William Heinemann Ltd
15 Queen Street, Mayfair, London W1X 8BE

LONDON MELBOURNE TORONTO
JOHANNESBURG AUCKLAND

434 29073 4

First published in Great Britain 1963
Reprinted 1966, 1970, 1972
Reset 1974
Copyright © 1962 by Anthony R. Ferris

Filmset and printed Offset Litho in Great Britain
by Cox & Wyman Ltd
London, Fakenham and Reading

CONTENTS

PREFACE

It is in tribute to Kahlil Gibran's love for beauty in thought and expression, and to his devotion to art that I have translated this new collection of his prophetic sayings and parables. To the millions of English-speaking admirers of the author of *The Prophet* I am happy to provide more fruit from the spiritual garden of a soul rich in faith and beneficence.

Among them will be found some of the bitter but incisive writings of Gibran from the period of his exile from his country and excommunication from his church. Many years later he was recalled from exile, and the church embraced him. He wrote voluminously, enriching more than thirty nations with his unique literary and artistic productions. He retained his lofty non-denominational devotion to the spirit and to ethics. To those who may be reading Gibran for the first time it may be pointed out that he combines almost frighteningly vivid perceptions of spiritual reality with an exquisite, lacy poetry. Its originality and power have won admiration and even reverence from millions of readers in dozens of languages. He has won almost equal acclaim as an artist. His drawings and paintings are exhibited periodically in world metropolises. When the great Rodin desired his portrait painted, Gibran, who is compared to him and to William Blake, was commissioned as the artist. In the Western world this poet, philosopher, and artist is called the Dante of the twentieth century; by Orientals he is fondly termed the Beloved Master.

A mourner at the Gibran funeral procession in 1931 described it as beyond imagination. Hundreds of priests and religious leaders, representing every denomination under Eastern skies, were in solemn attendance. Included were Maronite Catholics, Shiites, Protestants, Mohammedans, Greek Orthodox, Jews, Sunnites, Druses, and others. And to render complete Gibran's restoration to the church fold, he was buried in the grotto of the Monastery of Mar Sarkis in Bcherri, Lebanon, the church of his Childhood.

ANTHONY R. FERRIS

Austin, Texas

SPIRITUAL SAYINGS

OF

KAHLIL GIBRAN

SAYINGS

I discovered the secret of the sea in meditation upon the dewdrop.

★ ★ ★

Where can I find a man governed by reason instead of habits and urges?

★ ★ ★

As one's gifts increase, his friends decrease.

★ ★ ★

If you are poor, shun association with him who measures men with the yardstick of riches.

★ ★ ★

I prefer to be a dreamer among the humblest, with visions to be realized, than lord among those without dreams and desires.

★ ★ ★

Of life's two chief prizes, beauty and truth, I found the first in a loving heart and the second in a labourer's hand.

People speak of plague with fear and tremor, yet of destroyers like Alexander and Napoleon they speak with ecstatic reverence.

★ ★ ★

Thrift is being generous, to all except the misers.

★ ★ ★

I saw them eating and I knew who they were.

★ ★ ★

No lower can a man descend than to interpret his dreams into gold and silver.

★ ★ ★

Someone said to a stubborn prattler, "Your conversation soothes and cures the ailing heart." Whereat he hushed and claimed to be a medical doctor.

★ ★ ★

What shall I say of the man who slaps me when I kiss him on the face and who kisses my foot when I slap him?

★ ★ ★

How hard is the life of him who asks for love and receives passion!

★ ★ ★

To be closer to God, be closer to people.

4

Marriage is either death or life; there is no betwixt and between.

* * *

Keep me from the man who says, "I am a candle to light people on their way"; but to the one who seeks to make his way through the light of the people, bring me nearer.

* * *

It is slavery to live in the mind unless it has become part of the body.

* * *

Some silky faces are lined with coarse cloth.

* * *

Some think I wink at them when I shut my eyes to avoid their sight.

* * *

My proof convinces the ignorant, and the wise man's proof convinces me. But he whose reasoning falls between wisdom and ignorance, I neither can convince him, nor can he convince me.

* * *

If reward is the goal of religion, if patriotism serves self-interest, and if education is pursued for advancement, then I would prefer to be a non-believer, a non-patriot, and a humbly ignorant man.

An epoch will come when people will disclaim kinship with us as we disclaim kinship with the monkeys.

★ ★ ★

Some hear with their ears, some with their stomachs, some with their pockets; and some hear not at all.

★ ★ ★

Some souls are like sponges. You cannot squeeze anything out of them except what they have sucked from you.

★ ★ ★

If there were two men alike, the world would not be big enough to contain them.

★ ★ ★

This is the history of man: birth, marriage, and death; and birth, marriage, and death; and birth, marriage, and death. But then a madman with strange ideas appears before the people and tells a dream of a different world whose more cultured beings see more in their dreams than birth, marriage, and death.

★ ★ ★

He brings disaster upon his nation who never sows a seed, or lays a brick, or weaves a garment, but makes politics his occupation.

6

By adornment one acknowledges his ugliness.

★　★　★

They say that silence resides in contentment; but I say to you that denial, rebellion, and contempt dwell in silence.

★　★　★

I have yet to meet an ignorant man whose roots are not embedded in my soul.

★　★　★

Truth is the daughter of Inspiration; analysis and debate keep the people away from Truth.

★　★　★

He who forgives you for a sin you have not committed forgives himself for his own crime.

★　★　★

The foundling is an infant whose mother conceived him between love and faith, and gave birth to him between the fear and frenzy of death. She swaddled him with a living remnant of her heart and placed him at the orphanage gate and departed with her head bent under the heavy burden of her cross. And to complete her tragedy, you and I taunted her: "What a disgrace, what a disgrace!"

★　★　★

Ambition is a sort of work.

The partition between the sage and the fool is more slender than the spider web.

★ ★ ★

Some seek pleasure in pain; and some cannot cleanse themselves except with filth.

★ ★ ★

The fear of hell is hell itself, and the longing for paradise is paradise itself.

★ ★ ★

We must not forget that there are still cave dwellers; the caves are our hearts.

★ ★ ★

We may change with the seasons, but the seasons will not change us.

★ ★ ★

Three things I like in literature: rebellion, perfection, and the abstract. And the three things I hate in it are imitation, distortion, and complexity.

★ ★ ★

If you choose between two evils, let your choice fall on the obvious rather than the hidden, even though the first appears greater than the second.

★ ★ ★

Deliver me from him who does not tell the truth

unless he stings; and from the man of good conduct and bad intentions; and from him who acquires self-esteem by finding fault in others.

★ ★ ★

Does the song of the sea end at the shore or in the hearts of those who listen to it?

★ ★ ★

The rich claim kinship with those of noble birth; and the nobly-born seek marriages among the rich; and each despises the other.

★ ★ ★

Most of us hover dubiously between mute rebellion and prattling submission.

★ ★ ★

The ill-intentioned always fall short of achieving their purpose.

★ ★ ★

The supreme state of the soul is to obey even that against which the mind rebels. And the lowest state of the mind is to revolt against that which the soul obeys.

★ ★ ★

They feed me the milk of their sympathy; if only they knew that I was weaned of such pap from the day of my birth.

9

The spiritual man is he who has experienced all earthly things and is in revolt against them.

★ ★ ★

Strange that virtue in me brings me nothing but harm, while my evil has never been to my disadvantage. Nevertheless, I continue fanatic in my virtue.

★ ★ ★

Oh, heart, if the ignorant say to you that the soul perishes like the body, answer that the flower perishes, but the seeds remain. This is the law of God.

★ ★ ★

If you wish to see the valleys, climb to the mountain top; if you desire to see the mountain top, rise into the cloud; but if you seek to understand the cloud, close your eyes and think.

★ ★ ★

Life kisses us on both cheeks
Day and morn,
But laughs at our deeds
Eve and dawn.

★ ★ ★

Listen to the woman when she looks at you, but not when she talks to you.

Affection is the youth of the heart, and thought is the heart's maturity; but oratory is its senility.

★ ★ ★

Which one of us listens to the hymn of the brook when the tempest speaks?

★ ★ ★

Hard is life for him who desires death but lives on for the sake of his beloved ones.

★ ★ ★

I was wandering in unexplored places of the earth when I was seized and made a slave. Then I was freed and became an ordinary citizen, and, in turn, a merchant, a scholar, a minister, a king, a tyrant. After being dethroned I became a rioter, a hoodlum, an impostor, a vagrant, then a slave lost in the unexplored realm of my soul.

★ ★ ★

As between the soul and the body there is a bond, so are the body and its environment linked together.

★ ★ ★

Be not contented with little; he who brings to the springs of life an empty jar will return with two full ones.

He who looks upon us through the eyes of God will see our naked and essential reality.

★　★　★

God made Truth with many doors to welcome every believer who knocks on them.

★　★　★

The flower that grows above the clouds will never wither. And the song chanted by the lips of the brides of dawn will never vanish.

★　★　★

He who philosophizes is like a mirror that reflects objects that it cannot see, like a cave that returns the echo of voices that it does not hear.

★　★　★

The poet is he who makes you feel, after reading his poem, that his best verses have not yet been composed.

★　★　★

The tyrant calls for sweet wine from sour grapes.

★　★　★

Who among men can stroll on the bottom of the sea as if promenading in a garden?

★　★　★

Do you believe you can comprehend the substances

by inquiring about the purposes? Can you tell the flavour of the wine by looking at the wine jug?

★ ★ ★

From my obscurity came forth a light and illuminated my path.

★ ★ ★

Our souls traverse spaces in Life which are not measurable by Time, that invention of man.

★ ★ ★

He who reveals to himself what his conscience has prohibited commits a sin. And he also is a sinner who denies himself what his conscience has revealed.

★ ★ ★

Poetry is the secret of the soul; why babble it away in words?

★ ★ ★

Poetry is the understanding of the whole. How can you communicate it to him who understands but the part?

★ ★ ★

Poetry is a flame in the heart, but rhetoric is flakes of snow. How can flame and snow be joined together?

13

How gravely the glutton counsels the famished to bear the pangs of hunger.

★ ★ ★

Representative governments were, in the past, the fruits of revolutions; today they are economic consequences.

★ ★ ★

A feeble nation weakens its strong ones and strengthens the weak ones of a powerful nation.

★ ★ ★

The heartbreak of love sings, the sadness of knowledge speaks, the melancholy of desire whispers, and the anguish of poverty weeps. But there is a sorrow deeper than love, loftier than knowledge, stronger than desire, and more bitter than poverty. It is mute and has no voice; its eyes glitter like stars.

★ ★ ★

The secret in singing is found between the vibration in the singer's voice and the throb in the hearer's heart.

★ ★ ★

Love is a trembling happiness.

★ ★ ★

A singer cannot delight you with his singing unless he himself delights to sing.

14

When, in misfortune, you seek commiseration from your neighbour, you give him a part of your heart. If he is good-hearted, he will thank you; if he is hard-hearted, he will scorn you.

★ ★ ★

You progress not through improving what has been done, but reaching toward what has yet to be done.

★ ★ ★

A sage met with a stupid magnate and they discussed education and wealth. When they separated, the sage found naught in his hand save a handful of dirt, and the magnate discovered nothing in his heart but a puff of mist.

★ ★ ★

The truth that needs proof is only half true.

★ ★ ★

Keep me from the wisdom that does not weep, and the philosophy that does not laugh, and the pride that does not bow its head before a child.

★ ★ ★

Among the people there are killers who have not yet shed blood, and thieves who have stolen nothing, and liars who have so far told the truth.

At ebb tide I wrote
A line upon the sand
And gave it all my heart
And all my soul.
At flood tide I returned
To read what I had inscribed
And found my ignorance upon the shore.

* * *

He is short-sighted who looks only on the path he treads and the wall on which he leans.

* * *

They think virtue is that which harasses me and relieves my neighbour, and sin that which relieves me and harasses my neighbour. Let them know that I can be either saint or sinner away from them in my hermitage.

* * *

Examine your yesterday's ledger and you will find that you are still indebted to people and to life.

* * *

Tenderness and kindness are not signs of weakness and despair, but manifestations of strength and resolution.

* * *

Poverty may veil arrogance, and the pain of calamity may seek the mask of pretence.

The hungry savage picks a fruit from the tree and eats it. The hungry citizen in civilized society buys a fruit from the one who bought it from another who bought it from him who picked it from the tree.

★ ★ ★

When I planted my pain in the field of patience it bore fruit of happiness.

★ ★ ★

Art is a step in the known toward the unknown.

★ ★ ★

THE NINE WOES

Woe to the nation that departs from religion to belief, from country lane to city alley, from wisdom to logic.

Woe to the nation that does not weave what it wears, nor plant what it eats, nor press the wine that it drinks.

Woe to the conquered nation that sees the victor's pomp as the perfection of virtue, and in whose eyes the ugliness of the conqueror is beauty.

Woe to the nation that combats injury in its dream but yields to the wrong in its wakefulness.

Woe to the nation that does not raise its voice save in a funeral, that shows esteem only at the grave, that waits to rebel until its neck is under the edge of the sword.

Woe to the nation whose politics is subtlety, whose philosophy is jugglery, whose industry is patching.

Woe to the nation that greets a conqueror with fife and drum, then hisses him off to greet another conqueror with trumpet and song.

Woe to the nation whose sage is voiceless, whose champion is blind, whose advocate is a prattler.

Woe to the nation in which each tribe claims to be a nation.

★ ★ ★

Education sows not seeds in you, but makes your seeds grow.

★ ★ ★

You eat in a hurry but are leisurely when you walk. Why, then, don't you eat with your feet and walk on the palms of your hand?

★ ★ ★

On the scholar who was made of thought and affection, speech was bestowed. On the researcher who was made of speech, a little thought and affection were bestowed.

★ ★ ★

Enthusiasm is a volcano on whose top never grows the grass of hesitation.

★ ★ ★

The millstone may break down but the river continues its course to the sea.

Inspiration is in seeing a part of the whole with the part of the whole in you.

★ ★ ★

Contradiction is the lowest form of intelligence.

★ ★ ★

The believer is led to doubt justice when he sees the trick of the fox triumph over the justice of the lion.

★ ★ ★

Fear of the devil is one way of doubting God.

★ ★ ★

Slaves are the faults of the kings.

★ ★ ★

The difficulty we meet with in reaching our goal is the shortest path to it.

★ ★ ★

They tell me, "If you find a slave asleep, don't wake him up; he may be dreaming of freedom." And I reply, "If you find a slave asleep, wake him and talk to him about freedom."

★ ★ ★

In the magnifying glass of man's eye the world looks greater than it is.

When the earth exhales it gives birth to us. When it inhales death is our lot.

★ ★ ★

That which we call intelligence in the mind of some people is but a local inflammation.

★ ★ ★

Art arises when the secret vision of the artist and the manifestation of nature agree to find new shapes.

★ ★ ★

Martyrdom is the voluntary falling of the supreme soul to the level of the fallen one.

★ ★ ★

Compulsion is a mirror in which he who looks for long will see his inner self endeavouring to commit suicide.

★ ★ ★

That which you think is ugly is but the treachery of the outer directed at the inner self.

★ ★ ★

We are all practical in our own interest and idealists when it concerns others.

★ ★ ★

I pity him whose lips and tongue writhe with words of praise while his hand is outstretched in beggary.

20

He is virtuous who does not acquit himself of the people's faults.

★ ★ ★

To realize that prophecy in the people is like fruit in the tree is to know the unity of life.

★ ★ ★

History does not repeat itself except in the minds of those who do not know history.

★ ★ ★

Evil is an unfit creature, laggard in obeying the law of the continuity of fitness.

★ ★ ★

Why do some people scoop from your sea and boast of their rivulet?

★ ★ ★

He is free who carries the slave's burden with patience.

★ ★ ★

Beauty in the heart that longs for it is more sublime than in the eyes of him who sees it.

★ ★ ★

Every innovator is a reformer. If he is right, he leads the people to the right path. If he is wrong, the fanaticism he rouses in them heartens them to stand for their right.

21

Sayings remain meaningless until they are embodied in habits.

★ ★ ★

The necessity for explanation is a sign of weakness in the text.

★ ★ ★

Faith is a knowledge within the heart, beyond the reach of proof.

★ ★ ★

Humanity is divinity divided without and united within.

★ ★ ★

He who comes clothed in his best at his neighbour's funeral will wear rags at his son's wedding.

★ ★ ★

According to the Arabic proverb, there are no such things as a Phoenix, a Ghoul, or a True Bosom Friend; but I say to you that I found them all among my neighbours.

★ ★ ★

The creator gives no heed to the critic unless he becomes a barren inventor.

Prosperity comes through two things: exploitation of the earth and distribution of its produce.

* * *

The just is close to the people's hearts, but the merciful is close to the heart of God.

* * *

Irregularity comes either from madness or from ingenuity.

* * *

He who pities woman depreciates her. He who attributes to her the evils of society oppresses her. He who thinks her goodness is of his goodness and her evil of his evil is shameless in his pretensions. But he who accepts her as God made her does her justice.

* * *

Poverty is a temporary fault, but excessive wealth is a lasting ailment.

* * *

Remembrance is a tripping stone in the path of Hope.

* * *

Our worst fault is our preoccupation with the faults of others.

I never speak without error, for my thoughts come from the world of abstraction and my statements from the world of reference.

★ ★ ★

Poetry is a flash of lightning; it becomes mere composition when it is an arrangement of words.

★ ★ ★

Had it not been for seeing and hearing, light and sound would have been naught but confusion and pulsations in space. Likewise, had it not been for the heart you love, you would have been a fine dust blown and scattered by the wind.

★ ★ ★

Passionate love is a quenchless thirst.

★ ★ ★

No one believes the sincere except the honest.

★ ★ ★

If you wish to understand a woman, watch her mouth when she smiles; but to study a man, observe the whiteness of his eyes when he is angry.

★ ★ ★

THE ARTS OF THE NATIONS

The art of the Egyptians is in the occult.
The art of the Chaldeans is in calculation.
The art of the Greeks is in proportion.

The art of the Romans is in echo.

The art of the Chinese is in etiquette.

The art of the Hindus is in the weighing of good and evil.

The art of the Jews is in the sense of doom.

The art of the Arabs is in reminiscence and exaggeration.

The art of the Persians is in fastidiousness.

The art of the French is in finesse.

The art of the English is in analysis and self-righteousness.

The art of the Spaniards is in fanaticism.

The art of the Italians is in beauty.

The art of the Germans is in ambition.

The art of the Russians is in sadness.

★ ★ ★

Someone gave me a lamb and I gave him a she-camel. Then he offered me two lambs and I repaid him with two she-camels. Later he came to my sheep-fold and counted my nine camels. Then he gave me nine lambs.

★ ★ ★

The most useful among the people is he who is distant from the people.

★ ★ ★

Your self consists of two selves; one imagines that he knows himself and the other that the people know him.

Science and religion are in full accord, but science and faith are in complete discord.

★ ★ ★

Subjects are the most anxious to learn about kings.

★ ★ ★

Nursing a patient is a sort of embalming.

★ ★ ★

If existence had not been better than non-existence, there would have been no being.

★ ★ ★

When you attain your pilgrimage, you will see everything beautiful even in eyes that never saw beauty.

★ ★ ★

I shall cast my jewels to the pigs so that they may swallow them and die either of gluttony or indigestion.

★ ★ ★

Can one sing whose mouth is full of filth?

★ ★ ★

When affection withers, it intellectualizes.

★ ★ ★

Poets are two kinds: an intellectual with an

26

acquired personality, and an inspired one who was a self before his human training began. But the difference between intelligence and inspiration in poetry is like the difference between sharp fingernails that mangle the skin and ethereal lips that kiss and heal the body's sores.

★ ★ ★

To understand the heart and mind of a person, look not at what he has already achieved, but at what he aspires to do.

★ ★ ★

He who stares at the small and near images will have difficulty in seeing and distinguishing those that are great and remote.

★ ★ ★

I am abashed by eulogies, but the eulogist rants on and makes me appear shameless before the whole world.

★ ★ ★

When I meditated upon Jesus I always saw him either as an infant in the manger seeing His mother Mary's face for the first time, or, staring from the crucifix at His mother Mary's face for the last time.

★ ★ ★

We are all warriors in the battle of Life, but some lead and others follow.

Souls are fires whose ashes are the bodies.

★ ★ ★

The pen is a sceptre, but how scarce kings are among the writers!

★ ★ ★

He who conceals his intention behind flowery words of praise is like a woman who seeks to hide her ugliness behind cosmetics.

★ ★ ★

If I knew the cause of my ignorance, I would be a sage.

★ ★ ★

The butterfly will continue to hover over the field and the dewdrops will still glitter upon the grass when the pyramids of Egypt are levelled and the sky-scrapers of New York are no more.

★ ★ ★

How can we hear the song of the field while our ears have the clamour of the city to swallow?

★ ★ ★

Trading is thieving unless it is barter.

★ ★ ★

The best of men is he who blushes when you praise him and remains silent when you defame him.

The pain that accompanies love, invention, and responsibility also gives delight.

★　★　★

What a man reveals differs from what he conceals as rain that falls over the fields differs from the cloud that looms over the mountains.

★　★　★

The chemist who can extract from his heart's elements compassion, respect, longing, patience, regret, surprise, and forgiveness and compound them into one can create that atom which is called LOVE.

★　★　★

He who requires urging to do a noble act will never accomplish it.

★　★　★

The strong grows in solitude where the weak withers away.

★　★　★

They say if one understands himself, he understands all people. But I say to you, when one loves people, he learns something about himself.

★　★　★

No one has prevented me from doing something who is not himself interested in it.

29

Fame burdens the shoulders of an excellent man, and by the way he carries the load people judge him. If he carries his burden unhaltingly he will be promoted to the rank of hero; but if his foot slips and he falls, he is counted among the impostors.

★ ★ ★

The optimist sees the rose and not its thorns; the pessimist stares at the thorns, oblivious of the rose.

★ ★ ★

Wishes and desires are Life's occupation. We must strive to realize Life's wishes and execute its desires whether we will or no.

★ ★ ★

He who fails to understand Socrates' character is spellbound by Alexander; when he cannot comprehend Virgil, he praises Caesar; if his mind cannot discern Laplace's thought, he blows his horn and beats his drum for Napoleon. And I have taken note that in the minds of those who admire Alexander, Caesar, or Napoleon I always found a touch of servitude.

★ ★ ★

When man invents a machine, he runs it; then the machines begin to run him, and he becomes the slave of his slave.

The virtue of some of the rich is that they teach us to despise wealth.

* * *

Oratory is the cunning of the tongue over the ear, but eloquence is the joining of the heart with the soul.

* * *

Civilization commenced when man first dug the earth and sowed seeds.

* * *

Religion began when man discerned the sun's compassion on the seeds which he sowed in the earth.

* * *

Art began when man glorified the sun with a hymn of gratitude.

* * *

Philosophy began when man ate the produce of the earth and suffered indigestion.

* * *

Man's value is in the few things he creates and not in the many possessions he amasses.

* * *

There is no true wealth beyond a man's need.

Every nation is responsible for each act of its individuals.

★ ★ ★

Who can separate himself from his sorrows and solitude without suffering in his heart?

★ ★ ★

Because voice need not carry the tongue and the lips on its wings, it penetrates the sky; so, too, the eagle need not carry its nest, but soars alone in the spacious firmament.

★ ★ ★

Love knows not its depth till the hour of separation.

★ ★ ★

Faith perceives Truth sooner than Experience can.

★ ★ ★

Most writers mend their tattered thoughts with patches from dictionaries.

★ ★ ★

Inhibitions and religious prohibitions do more harm than anarchy.

★ ★ ★

The nets of the law are devised to catch small criminals only.

32

Feigned modesty is imprudence adorned.

* * *

Courage, which is the sixth sense, finds the shortest way to triumph.

* * *

Chastity of the body may be miserliness of the spirit.

* * *

Keep me safe, Lord, from the tongue of the viper, and of him who fails to obtain the fame he craves.

* * *

I never met a conceited man whom I did not find inwardly embarrassed.

* * *

We fear death, yet we long for slumber and beautiful dreams.

* * *

Some who are too scrupulous to steal your possessions nevertheless see no wrong in tampering with your thoughts.

* * *

Our sorrow over the dead may be a sort of jealousy.

* * *

We all admire strength, but the majority is most impressed by it when it is without form and stability.

33

Few are those who respect strength when it is clearly defined and has meaningful ends.

★ ★ ★

The light of stars that were extinguished ages ago still reaches us. So is it with great men who died centuries ago, but still reach us with the radiations of their personality.

★ ★ ★

The sultan of sultans is he who has gained the love of the pauper.

★ ★ ★

There is no convenience in our present-day civilization that does not cause discomfort.

★ ★ ★

Your confidence in the people, and your doubt about them, are closely related to your self-confidence and your self-doubt.

★ ★ ★

We demand freedom of speech and freedom of the press, although we have nothing to say and nothing worth printing.

★ ★ ★

To you who praise the "happy medium" to me as the way of life, I reply, "Who wants to be lukewarm between cold and hot, or tremble between life and death, or be a jelly, neither fluid nor solid?"

34

Strength and tolerance are partners.

★　★　★

Love and emptiness in us are like the sea's ebb and flow.

★　★　★

Poverty hides itself in thought before it surrenders to purses.

★　★　★

Man merely discovers; he never can and never will invent.

★　★　★

Philosophy's work is finding the shortest path between two points.

★　★　★

Would it not be more economical for the governments to build asylums for the sane instead of the demented?

★　★　★

The most solid stone in the structure is the lowest one in the foundation.

★　★　★

When I wrote on my door:
"Leave your traditions outside,
Before you come in,"

35

Not a soul dared
To visit me or open my door.

★ ★ ★

Even the laws of Life obey Life's laws.

★ ★ ★

I learned to be daring from the indolence of my people.

★ ★ ★

He is most worthy of praise from whom the people unjustly withhold it.

★ ★ ★

The truly religious man does not embrace a religion; and he who embraces one has no religion.

★ ★ ★

Most men with delicate feelings hasten to hurt your feelings lest you precede them and hurt theirs.

★ ★ ★

The writer who draws his material from a book is like one who borrows money only to lend it.

★ ★ ★

When I didn't reward
One who eulogized me,
He grumbled and complained.
I suffered it in silence
And the people laughed at him.

36

Distinguish between the gift that is an insult and the gift that is a token of respect.

★ ★ ★

The one who disagrees is more talked about than the one who agrees.

★ ★ ★

I never doubted a truth that needed an explanation unless I found myself having to analyse the explanation.

★ ★ ★

Sweetness is closer to bitterness than it is to decay, no matter how sweetish its smell.

The essence of everything on earth, seen and unseen, is spiritual. On entering the invisible city my body is covered by my spirit. Who so seeks to cleave the body from the spirit, or the spirit from the body is turning his heart away from the truth. The flower and its fragrance are one; they are blind who deny the colour and the image of the flower, saying that it possesses only a fragrance vibrating in the ether. They are like those, deficient in the sense of smell, to whom flowers are nought but shapes and hues without fragrance.

Everything in creation exists within you, and everything in you exists in creation. You are in borderless touch with the closest things, and, what is more, distance is not sufficient to separate you from things far away. All things from the lowest to the loftiest, from the smallest to the greatest, exist within you as equal things. In one atom are found all the elements of the earth. One drop of water contains all the secrets of the oceans. In one motion of the mind are found all the motions of all the laws of existence.

★ ★ ★

God has placed in each soul an apostle to lead us upon the illumined path. Yet many seek life from without, unaware that it is within them.

★ ★ ★

In education the life of the mind proceeds gradually from scientific experiments to intellectual theories, to spiritual feeling, and then to God.

★ ★ ★

We are still busy examining sea shells as if they were all that emerge from the sea of life to the shore of day and night.

★ ★ ★

The tree that contrives to cheat life by living in the shade withers when it is removed and replanted in the sun.

★ ★ ★

Languages, governments, and religions are formed from the golden dust that rises from both sides of the road on which man's magnificent life proceeds.

The Spirit of the West is our friend if we accept him, but our enemy if we are possessed by him; our friend if we open our hearts to him, our enemy if we yield him our hearts; our friend if we take from that which suits us, our enemy if we let ourselves be used to suit him.

★　★　★

Exhaustion dooms every nation and every people; it is drowsy agony, death in a sort of slumber.

★　★　★

The potter can fashion a wine jug from clay, but nothing out of sand and gravel.

★　★　★

Wailing and lamentation befit those who stand before the throne of life and depart without leaving in its hands a drop of the sweat of their brows or the blood of their hearts.

★　★　★

We devour the bread of charity because we are hungry; it revives, then slays us.

★　★　★

How ugly is affection that lays a stone on one side of a structure and destroys a wall on the other side!

How savage is love that plants a flower and uproots a field; that revives us for a day and stuns us for an age!

★ ★ ★

The means of reviving a language lie in the heart of the poet and upon his lips and between his fingers. The poet is the mediator between the creative power and the people. He is the wire that transmits the news of the world of spirit to the world of research. The poet is the father and mother of the language, which goes wherever he goes. When he dies, it remains prostrate over his grave, weeping and forlorn, until another poet comes to uplift it.

★ ★ ★

The calamity of the sons lies in the endowments of the parents. And he who does not deny them will remain the slave of Death until he dies.

★ ★ ★

The tremors of people shaken by the storm of life makes them appear alive. But in reality they have been dead since the day of their birth; and they lie unburied and the stench of decay rises from their bodies.

★ ★ ★

The dead tremble before the tempest, but the living walk with it.

Strange are the self-worshippers, since they worship carrion.

★ ★ ★

There are mysteries within the soul which no hypothesis can uncover and no guess can reveal.

★ ★ ★

Because he was born in fear and lives a coward, man hides in the crevices of the earth when he sees the tempest coming.

★ ★ ★

The bird has an honour that man does not have. Man lives in the traps of his fabricated laws and traditions; but the birds live according to the natural law of God who causes the earth to turn around the sun.

★ ★ ★

Believing is one thing, doing another. Many talk like the sea but their lives are stagnant marshes. Others raise their heads above the mountain tops, while their souls cling to the dark walls of caves.

★ ★ ★

Worship does not require seclusion and solitude.

★ ★ ★

Prayer is the song of the heart that makes its way to the throne of God even when entangled in the wailing of thousands of souls.

41

God made our bodies temples for our souls, and they should be kept strong and clean to be worthy of the deity that occupies them.

★ ★ ★

How distant I am from the people when I am with them, and how close when they are far away.

★ ★ ★

People respect motherhood only when it wears the raiment of their laws.

★ ★ ★

Love, like death, changes everything.

★ ★ ★

The souls of some people are like school blackboards on which Time writes signs, rules, and examples that are immediately erased with a wet sponge.

★ ★ ★

The reality of music is in that vibration that remains in the ear after the singer finishes his song and the player no longer plucks the strings.

★ ★ ★

What shall I say about him who borrows from me the money to buy a sword with which to attack me?

My enemy said to me, "Love your enemy." And I obeyed him and loved myself.

★ ★ ★

The black said to the white, "If you were grey I would be lenient with you."

★ ★ ★

Many who know the price of everything are ignorant of its value.

★ ★ ★

Every man's history is written upon his forehead, but in a language none but he who receives revelations can read.

★ ★ ★

Show me your mother's face; I will tell you who you are.

★ ★ ★

I know his father; how do you expect me not to know *him*?

★ ★ ★

The freedom of the one who boasts of it is a slavery.

★ ★ ★

Some people do not publicly thank me in order to express their gratitude but to make public their perception of my talent in order to be admired themselves.

★　★　★

Good taste is not in making the right choice, but in perceiving in something the natural unity between its quantities and qualities.

★　★　★

The coarseness of some is preferable to the gentleness of others.

★　★　★

When people abhor what they cannot comprehend, they are like those burning with fever, to whom the choicest food is unpalatable.

★　★　★

I love the smooth-faced children; and also the bearded elders, if they have truly risen from the cradle and the swaddling band.

★　★　★

The wolf preys upon the lamb in the dark of the night, but the blood-stains remain to accuse him by day.

★　★　★

Persecution does not make the just man to suffer, nor does oppression destroy him if he is on the right side of Truth: Socrates smiled as he took poison, and

Stephen smiled as he was stoned. What truly hurts is our conscience that aches when we oppose it, and dies when we betray it.

* * *

The marching ages trample man's works; but they do not obliterate his dreams, nor weaken his creative impulses. These remain because they are part of the Eternal Spirit, though they hide or sleep now and then, imitating the sun at nightfall and the moon at dawn.

* * *

The young Lebanese woman is like a spring that gushes from the heart of the earth and flows through winding valleys. Since it cannot find an outlet to the sea, it turns into a calm lake that reflects upon its growing surface the glittering stars and the shining moon.

* * *

Have I not survived hunger and thirst, suffering and mockery for the sake of the truth which heaven has awakened in my heart?

* * *

Truth is the will and purpose of God in man.

* * *

I shall follow the path to wherever my destiny and my mission for Truth shall take me.

45

The man who inherits his wealth builds his mansion with money taken from the weak and the poor.

★ ★ ★

The last steps of the slaughtered bird are painful, involuntary and unknowing; but those who witness that grisly dance know what caused it.

★ ★ ★

He is a traitor who uses the Gospel as a threat to extract money . . . a hypocrite who uses the cross as a sword . . . a wolf disguised in a lamb's skin . . . a glutton who adores the tables more than the altars . . . a gold-hungry creature who runs after the rolling coin to the farthest land . . . a cheat who pilfers from widows and orphans. He is a monstrous being, with an eagle's beak, a tiger's claws, a hyena's teeth, and viper's fangs.

★ ★ ★

God has placed a torch in your hearts that glows with knowledge and beauty; it is a sin to extinguish that torch and bury it in the ashes.

★ ★ ★

God has created your spirits with wings to fly in the spacious firmament of Love and Freedom. How pitiful to lop off your wings with your own hands and suffer your spirit to crawl like vermin upon the earth.

46

THE PHILOSOPHY OF LOGIC

O NE rainy evening in the City of Beirut, Salem Effandy Daybis seated himself before a bookshelf in his study and began to turn over the pages of an old volume, puffing now and then from between his thick lips a cloud of smoke he drew from a Turkish cigarette. He was reading the dialogue on Self-Knowledge by Socrates, recorded by his disciple Plato.

Salem Effandy meditated on what he had read and felt full of praise for the philosophers and sages of the East and the West.

"Know thyself," he echoed Socrates, and jumped from his seat, raised his arms and exclaimed, "Indeed, I must know myself and penetrate into my secret heart, and thus will I cast off doubt and anxiety. It is my paramount duty to disclose my ideal being to my material being and then to disclose the secrets of my flesh-and-blood existence to my abstract essence."

Seized with unwonted fervour, his eyes glittered with love for knowledge—self-knowledge.

Then he went into the adjoining room and stood like a statue before a mirror, staring at his ghostly self and pondering upon the shape of his head and face, and the trunk and limbs of his body.

He remained in that position for half an hour as if

47

the Ethereal Knowledge were showering him with wonderful and exalted thoughts in which his soul's secrets were being unveiled, filling his heart with light. Then he calmly opened his mouth and addressed himself:

"I am short in stature, but so were Napoleon and Victor Hugo. I have a narrow forehead, but so had Socrates and Spinoza. I am bald-headed, but so was Shakespeare. My nose is long and crooked, but so were the noses of Voltaire and George Washington. I have sunken eyes, but so did Paul the Apostle and Nietzsche. My thick lips are similar to those of Louis XIV, and my thick neck is exactly like Hannibal's and Mark Anthony's."

After a moment's pause he resumed:

"My ears are long and might suit the head of an animal, but Cervantes had just such ears. My features are protuberant and my cheeks are hollow, but so were Lafayette's and Lincoln's. My chin recedes like that of William Pitt and Goldsmith. One of my shoulders is higher than the other, but Gambetta's shoulders were like that. The palms of my hands are too thick and my fingers are too short, and in this I resemble Eddington.

"My body is on the skinny side, but this is a characteristic common to great thinkers. Strange that I cannot settle down to read or write without having my coffee pot beside me like Balzac. Above all, I am inclined to associate with vulgar people, in which respect I resemble Tolstoy. Sometimes I go three or four days without washing my hands and face. So did Beethoven and Walt Whitman. Strange that I take time to relax and listen to the gossip of women about their behaviour when their husbands are away. This is exactly what Boccaccio did. My thirst for wine exceeds that of Marlowe, Abi Nowas and Noah, and my gluttony surpasses that of Emir Basheer and Alexander the Great."

After another pause Salem Effandy touched his forehead with the tips of his dirty fingers and continued:

"This is myself—this is my reality. I possess all the qualities of great men from the beginning of history to the present. A youth with such qualities is destined to great achievements.

"The essence of wisdom is such self-knowledge. Henceforth I shall start the great work for which I was delegated by the Great Thought of this universe, who planted in the depth of my heart certain visible elements. I have accompanied great men from the time of Noah down to Socrates, through Boccaccio, to Ahmad Farris Shidyak. I do not know what great deed I shall begin with, but a man who has united in his mystic self and real person all these mystic qualities fashioned by the hands of the days and the inspirations of the nights is undoubtedly capable of achieving great things. . . . I have known myself; yes, and the Deity has known me. Long live my soul, and long live myself. May the universe endure for ever that I may be able to achieve my purpose."

And Salem Effandy walked back and forth in the room, his ugly face shining with joy, and with a voice that sounded like the mewing of the cat in unison with the rattling of bones, he repeated this verse by Abi' Al-Ala' Al Ma'arri:

> *Although I am the last of this epoch,*
> *I shall bring forth what the*
> *founding fathers could not.*

And soon our friend was asleep in his untidy clothes upon his filthy bed, and his snore sounded like the grinding of millstones.

THE GREATER SEA

YESTERDAY—and how far yesterday is and how near it is!—my soul and I went to the great sea to wash off from our body the clinging mire of earth.

When we reached the shore we searched for a private place to escape the eyes of the people. And as we were walking along, we saw a man sitting upon a dusty brown rock holding a sack from which, every now and then, he would take out a handful of salt and sprinkle it in the sea.

And my soul said to me, "This man is a pessimist who sees nothing of life save its darkness. He is unworthy of beholding our naked bodies. Let us seek another place."

We continued our search until we reached an inlet. There we saw a man near a white rock holding a small box studded with precious stones. Every now and then he would take out of the box a lump of sugar and throw it into the sea.

And my soul said to me, "This is the optimist who seeks the impossible. Neither is such a man worthy of beholding our naked bodies."

And we continued our search until we came across a third man standing on the shore picking up small dead fish and throwing them back into the sea.

And my soul said to me, "This is the compassionate fool who endeavours to restore life to the dead. Let us keep away from him."

And we walked on until we saw a fourth one outlining his shadow upon the sand and the waves erasing his drawing.

And my soul said to me, "This is the mystic who erects from his imagination an idol to worship. Let us leave him."

Then we found a fifth man standing in a shallow, quiet lagoon, skimming the froth from the surface of the water and placing it in a carnelian vase.

And my soul said to me, "This is the idealist who weaves a garment for himself from the thread of the spider. He is not privileged to see our naked bodies."

And we resumed our march until we heard a loud voice saying, "This is the deep sea. This is the awful and the great sea."

Investigating the source of the voice, we traced it to a man whom we saw standing with his back toward the water. He had placed a shell over his ear and was listening to its grumbling.

And my soul said to me, "Let us depart, for this man is a sceptic who turns his back to the entirety which he is unable to encompass, and lets himself be directed by a trifle."

And we marched on until we saw a seventh man standing between two rocks with his head buried in the sand.

And I said to myself, "Oh, soul, let us bathe here, for this man cannot see us."

And my soul shook her head and said, "No, and a thousand times no. The man you see now is the most evil of all. He is the God-fearing man who hides himself from the tragedy of life while life hides her joys from him."

Then a deep sorrow appeared on the face of my soul, and with a pitiful voice she said, "Let us leave these shores, for there is no privacy here. I shall not let the wind play with my long, golden hair, or uncover my white bosom here. I will not strip myself and stand naked before the light."

And my soul and I left that great sea and walked together seeking the greater sea.

THE FEZ AND THE INDEPENDENCE

RECENTLY I read an article by a scholar protesting about the crew of a French steamer on which he sailed from Syria to Egypt. His complaint was that they had made him, or rather, endeavoured to make him remove his fez while eating at their table.

We all know that Occidentals consider it good manners to dine bareheaded. Our scholar's protest surprised me, for he re-emphasized the Oriental adherence to symbolic acts that, in their eyes, adorn their daily life. I was as struck by it as I once was when a Hindu prince refused my invitation to the opera in Milan. He said to me, "If you had invited me to visit Dante's Inferno I would have accepted the invitation with pleasure; but not the opera. I cannot sit in a place where I am obliged to remove my turban and smoke no cigarettes."

It pleases me when an Oriental adheres even to a shadow of the shadows of his customs and traditions. However, there are some harsh truths to consider.

If our scholar friend, who resented removing his fez while on a European boat, had considered that this noble headdress had been made in a European factory, he might have found it easier to remove it from his head.

Such independent self-assertion had better be asserted, first, in national industry and culture. Our scholar might have recalled that his Syrian forefathers used to sail to Egypt on a Syrian boat in garments spun, woven, and tailored by Syrian hands. It were better that he, too, wore clothes made in his country and sailed on a ship made and manned by Syrians.

The trouble with our scholar is that he protested against the outcome and disregarded the causes. This is the way of most Orientals who insist on being Oriental only in small and trifling matters, and boast of things they have taken over from the Occidentals which are not small or trifling.

To our scholar and to all the clan of fez wearers let me say this: "Make your fezzes at your own workshops; then decide what you would like to do with them while riding a boat or climbing a mountain, or entering a cave."

May heaven be my witness, I did not write this to start a discussion on whether to remove or wear a fez on any occasion. It has other objectives than any fez upon any head over any trembling body.

ASSILBAN

Place: Home of Yousif Mussirrah in Beirut.
Time: An evening in the spring of 1901.

Personages:

PAUL ASSILBAN, musician and writer.

YOUSIF MUSSIRRAH, writer and scholar.

HELEN MUSSIRRAH, Yousif's sister.

SALEM MOWAD, poet and lute player.

KHALIL BEY TAMER, government official.

The curtain rises over a salon in YOUSIF MUSSIRRAH's *mansion, a spacious, beautiful room on whose tables are strewn books, magazines, and newspapers.* KHALIL BEY TAMER *is smoking a Turkish pipe,* HELEN *is embroidering, and* YOUSIF MUSSIRRAH *is smoking a cigarette.*

KHALIL
(*Addressing* YOUSIF)

I read your article today on the Fine Arts and liked it very much. If it weren't for its European tone, I would acclaim it as the best I ever read. But I foresee evil in the influence of Western education.

YOUSIF

You may be right, my friend, yet your actions contradict your views. You wear European clothes, use Western utensils in your kitchen, and sit on European chairs. Above all, you spend more time reading Western literature than Arabic books.

KHALIL

These are superficial; they have no connection with real culture.

YOUSIF

Yes, they have a vital and essential connection. If you think more deeply on the subject, you will find that arts reflect and influence customs, styles, religious and social traditions—every aspect of our life.

KHALIL

I am an Oriental and I shall remain Oriental in spite of my European dress. It is my sincere wish that the Arabic literature remain free of European influences.

YOUSIF

Then would you condemn Arabic literature to extinction?

KHALIL

How does that follow?

YOUSIF

Old cultures that fail to revitalize themselves by the production of modern culture are doomed to intellectual death.

KHALIL

Where's your proof?

YOUSIF

I have a thousand proofs.

(*At this moment* PAUL ASSILBAN *and* SALEM MOWAD *walk in. Everybody rises in respect.*)

YOUSIF

Welcome to our home, brothers. (*Addresses* PAUL ASSILBAN) Welcome, oh nightingale of Syria.

57

(HELEN *looks at* PAUL *and her cheeks redden and signs of joy appear on her face.*)

SALEM

Please, Yousif, withhold your praise from Paul.

YOUSIF

Why?

SALEM

(*With mock seriousness*)

Because he has done something not worthy of honour and respect. He has given way to a strange mood; he is a madman.

PAUL

(*To* SALEM)

Did I bring you here to enlarge on my short-comings?

HELEN

What has happened, Salem? What new faults have you discovered in Paul?

SALEM

Not a new fault, but an old one carried to an extreme that makes it appear new.

YOUSIF

Tell us what happened.

SALEM

(*Speaking to* PAUL)

Would you prefer to have me speak of it, Paul, or do you want to confess it yourself?

PAUL

I would rather you remained silent as a grave or still as an old woman's heart.

Then I *shall* talk.

PAUL

I see, you are determined to spoil our evening.

SALEM

No, but I would like to tell our friends what happened so that they know the kind of man you are.

HELEN

(*Talking to* SALEM)

Tell us what happened. (*Addressing* PAUL) Perhaps the crime Salem wishes to expose will only demonstrate your virtues, Paul.

PAUL

I have neither committed a crime, nor attained a virtue; but what our friend is so anxious to discuss is not worthy of mention. Besides, I don't relish being made the text of an idle conversation.

HELEN

Good, let us hear the story.

SALEM

(*Rolls a cigarette and sits by* YOUSIF)

Gentlemen, you have undoubtedly heard of the wedding party Jalal Pasha held to celebrate the marriage of his son. He invited all the city's notables, including this rascal (*Pointing to* PAUL) and me, as well. The reason *I* was invited was the common belief that I am Paul's shadow, and, besides, Paul, bless his heart, does not care to sing unless I accompany him.

We arrived late, as is Paul's royal custom. There we found the Governor and the Bishop, the beautiful ladies and the scholars, the poets, the nabobs, and the chiefs.

As we sat down between the censers and the wine cups the guests gazed at Paul as if he were an angel descended from heaven. The beautiful ladies offered him wine and flowers as did the women of Athens to heroes returning from battle.

In short, our Paul was the object of honour and respect. . . . I took up my lute and played a while before Paul opened his mouth and sang a verse from Al Farid's poem. The audience was all ears as if El Moussoli had returned from Eternity to whisper in their ears a divine and magic air. Suddenly Paul stopped singing. The audience expected him to resume after easing his throat with some wine. But Paul remained silent.

PAUL

Stop. Don't go on with this nonsense. I'm sure our friends are not interested.

YOUSIF

Please let's hear the rest.

PAUL

It seems you people prefer his chatter to my presence. Goodbye.

HELEN

(*Looks at* PAUL *tenderly*)

Sit down, Paul; no matter what the story will be, we are all for you. (PAUL *sits down, resignedly*.)

SALEM

(*Resumes his talk*)

I said that poor Paul had sung one verse of Al Farid's

60

poem and stopped. This was tantamount to serving his poor, hungry listeners a morsel of the goddess' bread and then kicking the table down and breaking the vases and the cup. There he sat silent as the Sphynx on the sands of the Nile. The beautiful ladies rose from their seats, one after the other, and implored Paul to sing, but he refused, saying that he had a sore throat. Then the dignitaries came and beseeched him, but he remained as unyielding as if God had converted his heart into flint and his singing into coquetry. It was past midnight when Jalal Pasha called him to another room, put a heap of dinars in his hand and said, "Without your song the spirit of this party languishes. I beg you to accept this gift not as a reward, but as a token of my affection and admiration for you. Do not disappoint us." Paul threw down the dinars and said in the tone of a conquering king, "You insult me. I did not come here to sell myself; I came here as a well-wisher."

Losing his temper, Jalal Pasha uttered some coarse words and our sensitive Paul left the house cursing woefully. I picked up my lute and followed him, leaving behind the beautiful ladies and the banquet wine and food. I sacrificed all this for the sake of my stubborn friend, who has not even thanked me or praised me for my devotion to him.

YOUSIF
(*Laughing*)

This is really an interesting story, worthy of being written with needles upon the pupils of the eyes.

I have not finished. The most interesting part of it is to come. No Indian or Persian storyteller ever invented such a devilish ending.

PAUL

(*Addressing* HELEN)

I will stay for your sake, but please tell this frog to stop croaking.

HELEN

Let him talk, Paul; I assure you we are all on your side.

SALEM

(*Lights another cigarette and continues*)

We left Jalal Pasha's home with Paul cursing the rich, and me cursing Paul in my heart. But do you think we went home from Jalal Pasha's mansion? Listen and wonder! You all know that Habeeb Saadi's home is located opposite to Jalal Pasha's. Only a small garden separates them. Habeeb likes to drink, sing, and dream; and he worships this idol (*pointing to* PAUL). On leaving the Pasha's mansion, Paul stood for a few minutes in the middle of the street rubbing his forehead like a generalissimo planning a campaign against a rebellious kingdom. Then he suddenly walked to Habeeb's home and rang the doorbell. Habeeb appeared in his nightgown, rubbing his eyes, and yawning. On seeing Paul and me with my lute under my arm, his eyes glittered with joy as if heaven had opened its gates and brought us to him.

"What brought you here at this blessed hour?" said he to us. And Paul replied, "We come to celebrate

the wedding feast of Jalal Pasha's son at your home."
And Habeeb responded, "Is not the Pasha's home big
enough for you?" And Paul retorted, "The Pasha's
home has no true ears for our music and therefore we
have come to yours. Bring the *arak**★** and the
appetizers and ask no more questions."

We seated ourselves comfortably. When Paul had
finished his second drink, he opened all the windows
that faced Jalal Pasha's home, handed the lute to me
and said, "This is your staff, Moses; turn it into a
viper and play it long and well." I took my lute and
played it obediently. Paul turned his face toward the
Pasha's home and sang in the full range of his voice.

(SALEM *pauses, then resumes in a more serious tone.*)

I have known Paul for fifteen years. We went to
school together. I have heard him sing when he was
in a happy mood and in sadness. I have heard him
wail like a widow bereft of her only child; I have
heard him sing like a lover and chant like a victor. I
have heard him in the silence of the night voicing
whispers that enchanted the sleepers. I have heard
him sing in the valleys of Lebanon in unison with the
distant church bells and filling space with magic and
reverence. I have heard him sing a thousand times
and thought that I knew all his powers. But last
night, when he faced the Pasha's home and sang, I
said to myself, "How little I knew about this man's
life!" Now I begin to understand him. In the past
I only heard his tongue sing, but last night I heard his
heart and soul. . . .

★Lebanese brandy.

63

Paul sang one verse after the other. I felt that the lovers' souls were hovering over our heads, whispering, recalling the distant past, unfolding what the night had covered, of humanity's hopes and dreams. Yes, gentlemen, this man (*Pointing to* PAUL) scaled the ladder of art to its highest rungs last night, and reached the stars, and did not come down to earth until dawn. By then he had subdued his enemies and made them a stool for his feet. Hearing his voice, the Pasha's guests crowded to the windows and some came out and sat under the tree in the garden, forgiving this idol who vexed and insulted them while filling their hearts with divine and intoxicating melody. Some cheered him and praised him, while others cursed him. I learned from the guests that Jalal Pasha roared like a lion and paced the hall, back and forth, cursing Paul and reviling the guests who left the banquet to hear him. Well, now that you've heard the end, what do you think of this genius and madman?

KHALIL BEY

I don't blame Paul, for I don't presume to understand his secrets and intents; I know this is a personal matter that concerns him only. I realize that an artist's character, especially that of a musician, differs from the ordinary. It is not just to measure their actions with the common yardstick. The artist, and by artist I mean he who creates new images for his thoughts and affections, is a stranger among his people and even among his friends. He turns eastward when others turn westward. What affects him within, he himself does not understand. He is miserable among the merrymakers, and happy among the melancholy. He is weak among the capable and capable among the weak. He is above the law, whether people like it or not.

KHALIL

Your words, Yousif, do not differ in meaning from your article on the fine arts. Let me repeat: "The European spirit which you advocate will some day be our ruin as a people and as a nation."

YOUSIF

Do you attribute Paul's behaviour last night to the European influence you object to?

KHALIL

I am amazed at what Paul did, despite my respect for him.

YOUSIF

Doesn't Paul have the right and the freedom to do whatever he pleases with his art and music?

KHALIL

Yes, abstractly he has the right to do whatever he pleases; but it seems to me that our social system does not approve this kind of freedom. Our inclinations, customs, and traditions do not allow the individual to do what Paul did last night without exposing himself to criticism.

HELEN

Since the subject of this interesting debate is here, why not have him speak? I am sure that he will be capable of defending himself.

PAUL

(After a silence)

I wish Salem had not started this. What happened
last night is done with. But since I am now under
criticism, as Khalil said, I will give you my thoughts
on this subject.

You all know that I have long been under criticism.
I am said to be spoiled and capricious and undeserving
of honour. What can be the reason for such harsh
criticism? It is an attack on something in my character
which I cannot change, and would not if I could. It
is my independence, which refuses to be sold or
seduced by flattery. There are many singers and
musicians in this city; many poets, critics, and
scholars; many censer-bearers and beggars. They all
sell their voices, their thoughts and their conscience
for a coin, for a meal, for a bottle of wine. Our
nabobs and dignitaries buy artists and scholars cheap
and display them in their mansions as they display
their horses and carriages in the streets and parks.

Yes, the singers and poets in the Orient are little
better than slaves and censer-bearers. They are called
to sing at weddings, orate at banquets, lament at
funerals and eulogize over graves. They are like
talking machines of sorrow and joy. If the occasion
does not call for them, these machines will be set aside
like used utensils. I don't blame the rich; I blame the
singers, the poets, and the scholars who lack respect
for themselves. I blame them for not scorning the
petty and the trifling. I blame them for not preferring
death to humiliation.

KHALIL

(*Excited*)

But the guests and the host begged you to sing last night. How can you say your singing was a humiliation?

PAUL

If I had been able to sing at the Pasha's home last night I would have done so gladly. But looking around I could see only the rich, whose ears ring with the echoes of the almighty dinar, whose wisdom of life is to promote themselves at the expense of others. Such people could not differentiate between poetry and doggerel, between true music and tin pans. I will not make images to show to the blind, or utter the sounds of my soul to the deaf.

Music is the language of the spirit. Its hidden current vibrates between the heart of the singer and the soul of the listener. To those who cannot hear or understand, the singer cannot offer the contents of his heart. Music is a violin with taut and sensitive strings. If the strings loosen, they cannot function. The strings of my soul became loose last night when I looked at the guests in the Pasha's home. I saw nought but the false and the shallow, the stupid and the barren, the pretentious and the arrogant. They besought me to sing because I turned from them. Had I acted like the paid frog-singers, no one would have listened.

KHALIL

(*Joking*)

And after all you went to Habeeb's home to sing for spite from midnight until dawn.

I sang because I wanted to pour out my heart's content and to blame the night, Life and Time. I felt in dire need of tightening the strings of my soul that had become loose at the Pasha's home.

But if you think that it was done out of spite, you are free to say so. Art is a bird that soars freely in the sky or roams happily on the ground. No one can change its behaviour. Art is a spirit that cannot be bought or sold. We Orientals must learn this truth. Our artists—who are as scarce among us as red sulphur—should respect themselves, for they are vases filled with divine wine.

YOUSIF

I agree with you, Paul. This has taught me something new. You are a real artist, but I am a seeker and admirer of arts. The difference between us is like the difference between old wine and sour grapes.

SALEM

I am not convinced yet and I will never be convinced. Your philosophy is an ailment sprung from the foreign infection.

YOUSIF

If you heard Paul sing last night, you would not have called it an ailment.
(*At this moment the maid comes in and announces, "Refreshments are on the table."*)

YOUSIF

(*Rises from his seat*)

The *kanafe* is ready, and it is as sweet as Paul's voice.

(*All rise.* YOUSIF, KHALIL, *and* SALEM *leave the hall.*
PAUL *and* HELEN *linger to exchange sweet smiles and
ardent glances.*)

HELEN

(*Whispering*)

Did you know that I heard you sing last night?

PAUL

(*Surprised*)

What do you mean, Helen dear?

HELEN

(*Bashful*)

I was at my sister Mary's home when I heard you.
I spent the night there because her husband had left
town and she was afraid to stay by herself.

PAUL

Does your sister live at Pine Park?

HELEN

No, she lives across the street from Habeeb's home.

PAUL

And did you really hear me sing?

HELEN

Yes, I heard your soul's call from midnight until
dawn. I heard God speaking through your voice.

YOUSIF

(*Calls from the adjacent room*)

The *kanafe* is getting cold.

(HELEN *and* PAUL *leave the hall.*)

CURTAIN

YOUR LEBANON AND MINE

Y O U have your Lebanon and I have mine.

Yours is political Lebanon and her problems,
Mine is natural Lebanon in all her beauty,

You have your Lebanon with programmes and conflicts,
I have mine with her dreams and hopes.

Be satisfied with your Lebanon, as I am content with the free Lebanon of my vision.

Your Lebanon is a snarled political knot which Time endeavours to untie,

My Lebanon is a chain of knolls and mountains rising reverently and majestically toward the blue skies.

Your Lebanon is an international problem yet to be solved,

My Lebanon is calm, enchanted valleys murmurous with church bells and whispering brooks.

Your Lebanon is a contest between one from the West and an adversary from the South,

My Lebanon is a winged prayer that hovers in the morn when the shepherds lead their flocks to pasture, and again at eve when the peasants return from the fields and vineyards.

Your Lebanon is a census of countless heads,

Mine is a serene mountain sitting between the sea

and the plains like a poet between one eternity and another.

Your Lebanon is a trick of the fox when it encounters a hyena, and a ruse of the hyena when it encounters the wolf,

My Lebanon is a garland of memories of damsels exulting in the moonlight, and virgins singing between the threshing floor and the winepress.

Your Lebanon is a chess game between a bishop and a general,

My Lebanon is a temple in which my soul finds haven when she wearies of this civilization that runs on grating wheels.

Your Lebanon is two men—one who pays taxes and the other who collects them,

My Lebanon is one who leans his head upon his arm in the shadow of the Holy Cedars, oblivious to all save God and the light of the sun.

Your Lebanon is ports, posts, and commerce,

Mine is a distant thought and a flaming affection, and a divine word whispered by the earth into the ear of the space.

Your Lebanon is appointees, employees, and directors,

My Lebanon is the growth of youth, the resolution of maturity, and the wisdom of age.

Your Lebanon is representatives and committees,

My Lebanon is a reunion and gathering around the fireplace in the nights of tempest when darkness is assuaged by the purity of the snow.

Your Lebanon is parties and sects,

Mine is youth climbing rocky heights, wading in brooks, roving the fields.

Your Lebanon is speeches, lectures, and debates,

Mine is the singing of the nightingales, the rustling of the branches in the groves, the echoes of the shepherd's flute in the valleys.

Your Lebanon is disguises and borrowed ideas and deceit,

My Lebanon is simple and naked truth.

Your Lebanon is laws, rules, documents, and diplomatic paper,

Mine is in touch with the secrets of life which she knows without conscious knowledge; my Lebanon is a longing that reaches with its sensitive tip the far end of the unseen and believes it to be a dream.

Your Lebanon is a frowning old man, stroking his beard and thinking only of himself.

My Lebanon is a youth erect like a tower, smiling like dawn and thinking of others as he thinks of himself.

Your Lebanon seeks to be separate and at one with Syria at the same time.★

My Lebanon does not join or separate or swell or diminish.

You have your Lebanon and I have mine,

You have your Lebanon and her sons, and I have mine and her sons.

But who are the sons of your Lebanon?

Let me show you their reality:

★ Lebanon now is an independent republic separated from Syria. Gibran must have foreseen this separation fifty years ago.

They are those whose souls were born in the hospitals of the West, whose minds have wakened in the lap of the covetous playing the role of the generous.

They are like flexible branches that sway right and left. They tremble morn and eve, but are unaware of their trembling.

They are like a mastless and rudderless ship buffeted by the waves. Scepticism is its captain, and its port is a cave of goblins; for is not every capital in Europe a goblin cave?

These sons of Lebanon are strong and eloquent among themselves, but weak and mute among the Europeans,

They are free and ardent reformers, but only in the newspapers and on the platform.

They croak like frogs and say, "We are ridding ourselves of our old enemy," while their old enemy is hidden in their own bodies,

They march in a funeral procession singing and trumpeting, but greet a wedding cavalcade with wailing and rending of garments,

They know no hunger unless they feel it in their pockets. When they meet with one whose hunger is spiritual, they ridicule him and shun him saying, "He is but a ghost walking in a world of phantoms,"

They are like slaves who, because their rusty shackles have been replaced by glittering ones, consider themselves free.

Those are the sons of your Lebanon. Is there one among them as resolute as the rocks of Lebanon, as noble as the Lebanon mountains, as sweet and pure as the Lebanon water, as clean and fresh as the invigorating breeze of Lebanon?

Is there one among them who can claim that his life was a drop of blood in the veins of Lebanon or a tear in her eyes, or a smile upon her lips?

Those are the sons of your Lebanon. How great they are in your eyes, and how little in mine!

Now let me show you the sons of my Lebanon:

They are the peasants who turn the stony land into orchards and gardens.

They are the shepherds who lead their flocks from one valley to another that they may increase and multiply and offer to you their meat as food and their wool as raiment,

The sons of my Lebanon are the vinedressers who press the grapes and make good wine,

The fathers who raise mulberry trees and the mothers who spin the silk,

The husbands who harvest the wheat and the wives who gather the sheaves,

They are the masons and the potters, the weavers and the church-bell makers,

They are the poets and the singers who pour out their souls in new verses,

They are those who left Lebanon penniless for another country with hearts fired with enthusiasm and resolution to return with the plenty of the earth in their hands and the laurel wreaths of achievement adorning their brows,

They adapt to their new environment and are esteemed wherever they go,

These are the sons of my Lebanon, the unextinguished torches and the salt that cannot be corrupted,

They walk with sturdy feet toward truth, beauty, and perfection.

What will *you* leave for Lebanon and her sons a hundred years from today? Tell me, what will you leave for the future save pretence, falsehood, and stupidity?

Do you believe that the ether will store the ghosts of death and the breath of the graves?

Do you imagine that life smothers her body in rags?

Truly I say to you that the olive sapling planted by the villager at the foot of the mountain in Lebanon will outlast your deeds and achievements. And the wooden plough drawn by two oxen over the terraces of Lebanon outglories your hopes and ambitions.

I say unto you, and the conscience of the universe is my witness, that the chant of the vegetable picker on the slopes of Lebanon is worth more than the prattle of your notables.

Remember that you are naught. But when you realize your littleness, my aversion to you will change into sympathy and affection. It is a pity that you do not understand,

You have your Lebanon and I have mine,

You have your Lebanon and her sons. Be contented with her and them if you are happy with empty bubbles. As for myself, I am happy and comfortable with my Lebanon, and there is sweetness, contentment, and calm in my regard for her.

THE STORY OF THE VIRGIN

A flower no hand could touch,
she lived and died a virgin.

HIS forces were outnumbered and the general had no choice but to issue the following order:
"To avoid loss of life and ammunition we must retreat in an orderly manner to a town unknown to the enemy and there plan a new strategy. We shall march through the desert, for it is better to follow such a route than fall into the hands of the enemy. We will pass monasteries and convents which we shall occupy solely to obtain food and provisions."

The troops did not demur, for they saw no alternative in this critical situation.

They marched for days in the desert suffering fatigue, heat, hunger, and thirst. One day they saw an imposing structure that looked like an ancient fortress. Its gate was like that of a walled city. The sight of it brought cheer to their hearts. They thought it a convent where they could rest and find food.

When they opened the gate no one came to meet them, for a while. Then a lady dressed in black, her face the only visible part of her body, appeared at the door.

To the commanding officer she explained that the place was a nunnery and should be treated as such and no harm should be done to the nuns. The general promised full protection of the nuns and requested food for his troops. The men were served in the spacious garden of the convent.

The commander was a man of about forty years of age, vile, and incontinent. Tense with worry, he desired a woman to bring him relief and decided to force a nun. Thus, treacherous lust led him to pollute that sacred place where nuns had settled to commune with God and send Him unceasing prayers, far from the clamour of this false and corrupted world.

Having reassured the Mother Superior, the treacherous commander climbed a ladder that led into one of the rooms occupied by a nun he saw through the window. The years of continuous prayer and solitary self-denial had not effaced all marks of feminine beauty in her innocent face. She had come here as a refuge from the sinful world and as a place to worship God undistracted by the world.

On entering her room, the criminal drew his sword and threatened to kill her if she cried for help.

She smiled and was silent, acting as if willing to grant his wish. Then she looked at him and said, "Sit down and rest, you look very tired."

He sat near her, confident of his prey. And she said to him, "I wonder at you men of war, for not fearing when you fling yourselves in death's lap."

To which the stupid coward replied, "Circumstances oblige us to go to war. If people would not call me coward, I would run away before I consented to lead a damned army."

77

She smiled at him and said, "But don't you know that in this sacred place we have a salve which you can rub over your body to protect you from the blow of the sharpest sword?"

"Amazing! Where is this salve? I can surely use it."

"Good, I shall give you some of it."

Born in a time when people still believed in such superstitions, the general did not doubt the holy sister.

She opened a jar and showed him a white salve. On seeing it, he suddenly began to have doubts. She took a little of it and rubbed it on her neck and said to him, "If you do not believe me, I will prove it to you. Take your sword and strike my neck with all your might."

He hesitated, but she kept urging him to strike hard, and at last he did.

He came close to swooning when he saw the nun's head roll from her body, which fell motionless to the floor. Then he understood the ruse by which she had saved herself from defilement.

The nun was dead . . . and the commander could see nothing but two things in front of him: the virgin's corpse and the jar of salve. He began to stare now at the salve and then at the headless body. Then he lost his mind, pushed the door open and ran out, holding the bloody sword before him, crying aloud to his troops, "Hurry, hurry, let us leave this place!"

He did not stop running until some of his men reached him and found him crying like a senseless child, "I killed her! I killed her!"

YOUR THOUGHT AND MINE

YOUR thought is a tree rooted deep in the soil of tradition and whose branches grow in the power of continuity.

My thought is a cloud moving in the space. It turns into drops which, as they fall, form a brook that sings its way into the sea. Then it rises as vapour into the sky.

Your thought is a fortress that neither gale nor the lightning can shake.

My thought is a tender leaf that sways in every direction and finds pleasure in its swaying.

Your thought is an ancient dogma that cannot change you nor can you change it.

My thought is new, and it tests me and I test it morn and eve.

You have your thought and I have mine.

Your thought allows you to believe in the unequal contest of the strong against the weak, and in the tricking of the simple by the subtle ones.

My thought creates in me the desire to till the earth with my hoe, and harvest the crops with my sickle, and build my home with stones and mortar, and weave my raiment with woollen and linen threads.

Your thought urges you to marry wealth and notability.

Mine commends self-reliance.

Your thought advocates fame and show.

Mine counsels me and implores me to cast aside notoriety and treat it like a grain of sand cast upon the shore of Eternity.

Your thought instills in your heart arrogance and superiority.

Mine plants within me love for peace and the desire for independence.

Your thought begets dreams of palaces with furniture of sandalwood studded with jewels, and beds made of twisted silk threads.

My thought speaks softly in my ears, "Be clean in body and spirit even if you have nowhere to lay your head."

Your thought makes you aspire to titles and office.

Mine exhorts me to humble service.

You have your thought and I have mine.

Your thought is social science, a religious and political dictionary.

Mine is a simple axiom.

Your thought speaks of the beautiful woman, the ugly, the virtuous, the prostitute, the intelligent, and the stupid.

Mine sees in every woman a mother, a sister, or a daughter of every man.

The subjects of your thought are thieves, criminals, and assassins.

Mine declares that thieves are the creatures of monopoly, criminals are the offspring of tyrants, and assassins are akin to the slain.

Your thought describes laws, courts, judges, punishments.

Mine explains that when man makes a law, he either violates it or obeys it. If there is a basic law, we are all one before it. He who disdains the mean is himself mean. He who vaunts his scorn of the sinful vaunts his disdain of all humanity.

Your thought concerns the skilled, the artist, the intellectual, the philosopher, the priest.

Mine speaks of the loving and the affectionate, the sincere, the honest, the forthright, the kindly, and the martyr.

Your thought advocates Judaism, Brahmanism, Buddhism, Christianity, and Islam.

In my thought there is only one universal religion whose varied paths are but the fingers of the loving hand of the Supreme Being.

In your thought there are the rich, the poor, and the beggared.

My thought holds that there are no riches but life; that we are all beggars, and no benefactor exists save life herself.

You have your thought and I have mine.

According to your thought, the greatness of nations lies in their politics, their parties, their conferences, their alliances and treaties.

But mine proclaims that the importance of nations lies in work—work in the field, work in the vineyards, work with the loom, work in the tannery, work in the quarry, work in the lumberyard, work in the office and in the press.

Your thought holds that the glory of the nations is in their heroes. It sings the praises of Rameses, Alexander, Caesar, Hannibal, and Napoleon.

But mine claims that the real heroes are Confucius, Lao-Tse, Socrates, Plato, Abi Taleb, El Gazali, Jalal Ed-din-el Roumy, Copernicus, and Pasteur.

Your thought sees power in armies, cannons, battleships, submarines, aeroplanes, and poison gas.

But mine asserts that power lies in reason, resolution, and truth. No matter how long the tyrant endures, he will be the loser at the end.

Your thought differentiates between pragmatist and idealist, between the part and the whole, between the mystic and materialist.

Mine realizes that Life is *one* and its weights, measures and tables do not coincide with your weights, measures and tables. He whom you suppose an idealist may be a practical man.

You have your thought and I have mine.

Your thought is interested in ruins and museums, mummies and petrified objects.

But mine hovers in the ever-renewed haze and clouds.

Your thought is enthroned on skulls. Since you take pride in it, you glorify it too.

My thought wanders in the obscure and distant valleys.

Your thought trumpets while you dance.

Mine prefers the anguish of death to your music and dancing.

Your thought is the thought of gossip and false pleasure.

Mine is the thought of him who is lost in his own country, of the alien in his own nation, of the solitary among his kinfolk and friends.

You have your thought and I have mine.

Other books of prose and poetry by

KAHLIL GIBRAN

The Broken Wings

The Earth Gods, with five illustrations

The Forerunner, with five illustrations

The Garden of the Prophet, with six illustrations

Jesus, the Son of Man, with nine illustrations

The Madman, with three illustrations

Nymphs of the Valley, with four illustrations

The Prophet, with twelve illustrations

Prose Poems, with four illustrations

Sand and Foam, with five illustrations

A Self-Portrait

Spirits Rebellious, with four illustrations

A Tear and a Smile, with four illustrations

Thoughts and Meditations

The Voice of the Master

Spiritual Sayings

The Wanderer, with five illustrations